Earth's Biomes

Donna Latham

Chicago, Illinois

www.heinemannraintree.com
Visit our website to find out
more information about
Heinemann-Raintree books.

To order:
☎ Phone 888-454-2279
🖥 Visit www.heinemannraintree.com
to browse our catalog and order online.

©2009 Raintree
an imprint of Capstone Global Library, LLC
Chicago, Illinois

Edited by Adam Miller, Andrew Farrow, and
  Adrian Vigliano
Designed by Philippa Jenkins and Ken Vail
Original illustrations © Capstone Global Library
  Limited 2009
Illustrated by Maurizio De Angelis p13, 39;
  Gordon Hurden p16; Stephen Lings p35
Picture research by Ruth Blair
Originated by Raintree
Printed and bound in China by South China Printing
  Company Ltd

13 12 11 10 09
10 9 8 7 6 5 4 3 2 1

Library of Congress Cataloging-in-Publication Data
Latham, Donna.
  Earth's biomes / Donna Latham.
    p. cm. -- (Sci-hi. Life science)
  Includes bibliographical references and index.
  ISBN 978-1-4109-3329-4 (hc) -- ISBN 978-1-4109-
3337-9 (pb) 1. Biotic communities--Juvenile literature.
I. Title.
  QH541.14.L36 2009
  577--dc22
                        2009003569

Acknowledgments
The author and publishers are grateful to the following
for permission to reproduce copyright material:
Corbis/KOICHI KUMAGAI/amanaimages
p. **12**; naturepl.com pp. **9**, **15**, Georgette Douwma pp.
11 (top, bottom), Jeff Foott p. **28**, Laurent Geslin p. **4**,
Tony Heald p. **24**, Larry Michael p. **23**, David Noton
pp. **26**, **27**, Doug Perrine p. **39**, David Shale p. **37**,
Lynn M. Stone p. **31**, Staffan Widestrand p. **18**; NHPA/T
KITCHIN & V HURST p. **21**; Photolibrary pp. **2** (top,
bottom), **8**, **14**, **17**, **20**, **32**, **36**, **41**, **43**; Photolibrary/
Digital Vision p. **5**; Shutterstock/ © Stephanie Reynaud
p. **42**; Shutterstock: background images and design
features.

Cover photograph of the rain forest in Daintree
National Park, Queensland, Australia reproduced
with permission of Getty Images/Eric Jacobson **main**;
cover image of a Longluer frogfish reproduced with
permission of Corbis/Stephen Frink/zefa **inset**.

The publishers would like to thank literacy consultant
Nancy Harris and content consultant Michael Bright
for their assistance in the preparation of this book.

Contents

How does a barracuda's body shape allow it to hunt extra fast? Find out on page 36!

Some words are shown in bold, **like this**. These words are explained in the glossary. You will find important information and definitions underlined, <u>like this</u>.

What's a Biome?

Where do you live? Can you see a wooded area with towering oaks? Perhaps you hear waves crashing over a pebbly beach. Do mountains with snowy peaks rise in the distance? Or do you spot a tall cactus? It all depends on which **biome** you inhabit.

Plant life and soil

Earth is made up of different biomes. <u>**A biome is a large physical area where certain plant life grows.**</u> A biome contains a specific type of soil, which affects what plants grow there and how well they grow. In grasslands, for example, you'll find huge **pastures**. Low grasses thrive in rich soil. Grazing animals roam large open spaces. The tundra is different. There, you'll discover a super-short growing season. Some soil is permanently frozen. Plants perform special tricks to capture sunlight.

Terrestrial biomes, like the tundra, are located on land.

Climate, geography, and biodiversity

Within each biome is a particular range of species. This is called the **biodiversity** of that biome. <u>**Biodiversity is the range of living things in a community, ecosystem, or biome.**</u> Specific plant and animal communities inhabit different biomes. For example, in some grasslands with warm climates, you'll encounter zebras and kangaroos. In cold climates, you'll find snow leopards.

A biome has a particular geography and climate. For example, grasslands sprawl over every continent in the world except Antarctica.

The ocean is an aquatic, or underwater, biome.

What's the difference between climate and weather?

Have you heard the saying, "Climate is what you expect. Weather is what you get"? Climate is the average measure of weather patterns in an area over a specific period. Weather is the daily condition of Earth's atmosphere. For instance, you might live in a **temperate** (usually mild) region. It could experience hail today. Or the gloomy clouds could move along and let sunshine in.

Turn the page and locate your continent on the biome map.

The world's biomes

Take a look at this map. Did you find your continent? Now pinpoint your country and region. Use the map key to identify the biome in which you live.

Scientists don't agree about the total number of Earth's biomes. That's because scientists break biomes into smaller categories. Forest biomes, for example, include **coniferous** and **deciduous** forests. Coniferous trees include evergreens and produce needle-like leaves. Deciduous trees shed their leaves each year. They include tropical rain forests, too. <u>**Most scientists identify at least five major biomes: forest, grassland, desert, tundra, and aquatic.**</u>

In this book, we'll be discussing five major biomes. However, some scientists divide the world into many more biomes.

Terrestrial biome map

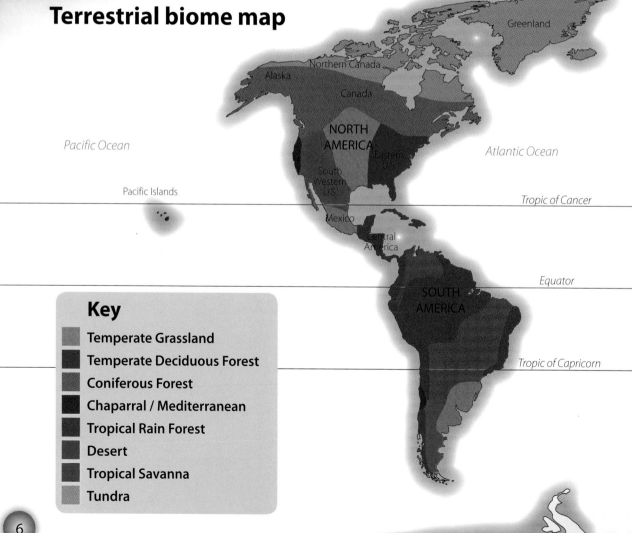

Greenland

Northern Canada

Alaska

Canada

NORTH AMERICA

Eastern U.S.

South Western U.S.

Pacific Ocean

Atlantic Ocean

Pacific Islands

Tropic of Cancer

Mexico

Central America

Equator

SOUTH AMERICA

Tropic of Capricorn

Key
- ■ Temperate Grassland
- ■ Temperate Deciduous Forest
- ■ Coniferous Forest
- ■ Chaparral / Mediterranean
- ■ Tropical Rain Forest
- ■ Desert
- ■ Tropical Savanna
- ■ Tundra

Distinct, yet connected

Biomes are separate and distinct. Yet, they are connected. What happens to one affects the others. <u>**Through natural processes or human activities, biomes can change.**</u> Overgrazed **savannas**, for example, can turn into deserts. Today's climate changes impact all Earth's biomes. Melting polar ice, for example, raises the levels in oceans. Higher sea levels cause floods.

In this book, you'll explore major biomes and smaller categories. You'll discover how human involvement changes biomes.

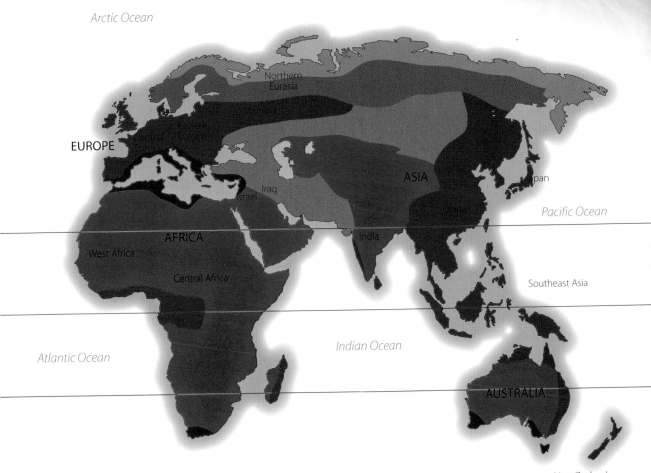

Adaptation

Consider your own area again. Which plants and animals are common? Saguaro cacti and iguanas? Douglas fir trees and bears? **Lichens** and caribou? Think of the foods available. Breadfruit? Prawns? Corn?

Adaptation

<u>**Through adaptation, animals and plants are perfectly suited for particular environments.**</u> That's why you'll never see an acacia tree and a harp seal in the same place. Do you live in the tundra? You won't share the area with a long-necked pink flamingo. The tropical bird couldn't survive the cold.

Adaptations are often physical. For example, sharp claws are perfect for burrowing animals, such as badgers and prairie dogs. They use claws to dig hideouts underground. Sharp claws come in handy for tigers, too. They use them to capture prey and to fight.

The jaguar of the tropical rain forest has spotted fur. This adaptation allows the meat-eater to prowl the forest floor in search of prey. Why? Furry spots blend in with areas of sunlight that penetrate the floor. That makes it easier for the jaguar to sneak up on its prey.

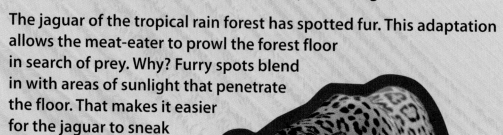

The jaguar's spotted fur blends in with sunny spaces.

In some dry parts of the world, trees have adapted by growing extra thick bark. This gives them a better chance of surviving a fire.

What's necessary for life in the water? Waterproof fur! Beavers and otters are aquatic mammals. Special fur on these great swimmers keeps them warm and lets water slip right off.

In some areas of the world that experience cold winters, trees have adapted sap with antifreeze compounds. In hot areas, adaptations are different. Cacti are covered with hairs or bristles, for instance, to act as shade. Waxy coatings on leaves keep water from escaping. In some exposed places, most plants grow low to the ground and in clusters to avoid high winds.

As you explore the **biomes**, you'll discover more about the special features plants and animals use for survival in different environments.

THREATS TO BIOMES

You've learned biomes are interconnected. When a change occurs in one, it affects others. Changes in Earth's temperature, for example, have impacted all the biomes. In the last hundred years, Earth's temperature increased by 0.5 °C (1 °F). It may not seem like much. Yet, it threatens natural areas. Read about some changes taking place in biomes around the globe.

Melting Arctic ice

In 2008, the United States government listed the polar bear as a threatened species. Many scientists believe the bear will eventually become endangered. It could even become **extinct**. Why? Polar bears are among the top predators in the Arctic food chain. The huge bears rely on ice platforms, which they use to hunt for seals. Yet, as Earth's temperatures increase, the Arctic ice melts earlier in spring and remains melted for longer periods of time. Polar bears may no longer be able to eat enough seals to store the fat supplies they need.

Warming and rising oceans

As Earth's temperatures increase, Arctic ice melts. So do glaciers. Gigantic ice shelves drop into oceans. What results? Ocean water levels rise. Small islands and their inhabitants get swept away. Coastal areas erode. In warming waters, phytoplankton decreases. These tiny plants are an important foundation of the food chain.

A healthy, living coral reef is full of color. Many sea plants and animals live there.

Coral reef bleaching

Coral is alive. It responds to stress caused by warming temperatures. How? It bleaches. When a coral reef bleaches, it releases algae **cells**. Algae are tiny, plantlike creatures. <u>Algae cells usually live inside coral as part of a symbiotic relationship. This means they benefit from each other.</u> Without the algae cells, bleached coral starves. It can die. When coral dies, entire reefs experience shifts in **biodiversity**.

Coral is also damaged by human actions. When people pollute waters with factory wastes or damage it through fishing methods, coral dies.

When people pollute coral reefs, it causes coral to bleach and die.

The Temperate Deciduous Forest

Locations:	Check the map on pages 6-7 to find Canada, China, central and eastern Europe, eastern United States, and Japan.
Characteristics:	Four seasons; rich soil; wide **biodiversity**
Rainfall:	762 mm—1,524 mm (30 to 60 inches)
Average Temperature:	10 °C (50 °F)
Threats:	**Acid rain** from air pollution, drought from climate change, habitat destruction

Forests occupy about one-third of Earth's **terrestrial** regions. They once covered much more. As the world's population increased, people cleared forests. They used trees as building materials. They made space for homes and businesses.

The **deciduous** forest is one category of the forest **biome**. You'll find deciduous forests in **temperate** climates. <u>A temperate climate experiences a full range of temperatures with four seasons.</u> Plants in the deciduous forest usually grow for half the year. In rich soil, vegetation grows in levels. Study the diagram on the next page as you read about each level.

Mature, tall trees form the first level of the forest.

Forest levels

Canopy
The tallest, oldest trees reach over other plants to capture as much sunlight as possible. Among them are birches, elms, maples, oaks, and pines.

Understory
From the canopy, sunlight penetrates the understory. Younger, smaller trees compete for space and light. Among them are dogwoods and holly.

Shrub Layer
Adapted to a level with limited light, bushes, shrubs, and herbs grow low to the ground. Dogbane, elderberries, and huckleberries are common.

Forest Floor
Decaying leaves, **lichens** (fungi and algae combining to make a plant), and mosses cover this dark, moist level. Worms, bacteria (tiny, single-celled organisms), and fungi move the **decomposing**, or rotting, process along.

POISON PLANTS!

"Leaves of three, let them be." The old saying warns people to steer clear of poison ivy. The pretty plant has waxy leaves, each with three leaflets, and is very common in deciduous forests. Poison oak is also common. Toxic to humans, the climbing vines cause rashes, swollen skin, and blisters. Scratching the rashes won't help. It will only spread it to other areas! Ouch!

Fall colors

Plants and animals are adapted to changing seasons. What does everyone know about deciduous forests? They have glorious fall colors! Do you live in a temperate climate? If you do, then you've observed the fall transformations of trees. Days become shorter and drier. **Chlorophyll**, a green pigment, breaks down. Leaves change to vibrant shades of red, orange, and gold. In time, they drop to the forest floor. They provide food for worms and bacteria.

During winter, trees and smaller plants fall **dormant**. In this inactive state, they stop growing. They spent all summer stashing extra food. Because of this **adaptation**, trees and plants live off stored food supplies until springtime.

People visit deciduous forests to enjoy beautiful fall colors.

In warmer months, bears store food, so they can hibernate from October to April. That's when forest food supplies are scarce.

Winter rests

How do forest animals adapt to winter's chill? When the environment changes, animals respond. Some change, too. Whitetail deer grow thicker coats. Small mammals cluster together for warmth. Others, including bears, **hibernate** over winter when food supplies are limited. They become dormant and appear to rest. Hibernating animals live off stored fat. Many birds, such as tiny warblers, **migrate** thousands of miles. They winter in a warmer forest biome, the tropical rain forest. *Read about the rain forest on page 16!*

Forest animals

In deciduous forests, there are plenty of animal species in a wide ranging biodiversity. Which are the main predators in this food web?

* Larger mammals, including bears, bobcats, coyotes, and wolves. They prowl among deer, raccoons, skunks, squirrels, wild turkeys, and chipmunks.

* Bluejays, hawks, and owls swoop through skies.

* Herons, geese, ducks, and fish inhabit ponds, streams, and lakes. So do frogs and toads.

* Lizards and snakes creep across forests floors and climb trees.

THE TROPICAL RAIN FOREST

Locations:	Check the map on pages 6-7 to find Australia, Central and South America, Pacific Islands, Southeast Asia, and West Africa.
Characteristics:	Hot and moist; most rainfall; greatest level of **biodiversity**
Rainfall:	2,032 mm–4,064 mm (80 to 160 inches)
Average Temperature:	25 °C (77 °F)
Threats:	Deforestation (destruction of forest) for farming, logging, and ranching

Direct rays

Why do birds **migrate** south to the rain forest? There's no winter in this **biome**. Tropical rain forests are close to the equator, where Earth is hottest. <u>Because of the way Earth curves, the Sun radiates from directly overhead at the equator.</u> At the poles, in contrast, the Sun remains low in the sky. It hits Earth with slanted rays. Temperatures are lower.

Sunlight, **precipitation** (forms of water that fall to the ground, like rain), temperature, and wind all contribute to a biome's climate. The tropical rain forest's climate is, well, tropical. It's hot and humid all year.

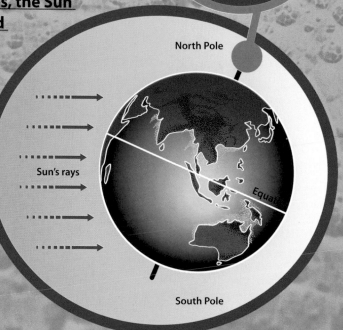

Earth's globe shape has a strong effect on temperatures around the world.

North Pole

Sun's rays

Equator

South Pole

Greatest level of biodiversity

Warm-to-hot temperatures and year-round rainfall mean rain forests enjoy a constant growing season. Vegetation is lush and varied. Tropical rain forests host the world's most amazingly wide-ranging **biodiversity. Rain forests cover only 6 percent of Earth's surface. Yet, 50 percent of the world's plant and animal species thrive in this biome.**

Did you know?

Over 7,500 butterfly species flit through the Amazon Rain Forest. Deforestation threatens the area, where 30 million people also live.

Deforestation for lumber and farmland greatly threatens the rain forest biome.

Leveled life

Like the deciduous forest, the rain forest grows in levels. The scattered emergent layer (taller than the surrounding vegetation) towers high. Some trees top 70 meters (250 feet). Waxy leaf surfaces keep trees from getting too dry beneath a scorching Sun.

Canopy

The dense canopy offers sunlight, shelter, and plenty of food. Trees reach 46 meters (150 feet). They provide safe homes for colorful parrots, gentle orangutans, and spider monkeys that feast on nuts and fruits. Tree frogs, spiders, and snakes hang around, too.

This level enjoys the most sunlight. Yet, it takes a beating from rainfall. How have plants adapted? Leaves grow pointy tips. Rainwater runs off quickly, so plants don't decay.

Camouflage

Camouflage is a natural disguise. Patterns and coloring allow animals to blend in with their environment. Take a peek at the photo of the three-toed tree sloths. Notice the algae and mold that grow in their brown fur? Green patches help the shy sloths to blend in with a tree. With this **adaptation**, the sloths hide from predators.

Three-toed sloths hide by blending in with a tree limb.

Understory

Little sunlight penetrates the humid understory. Saplings and shrubs grow in this darker, hotter level. So do palms and ferns. Plants adapt with broad leaves. They snatch as much light as possible.

Insect life, especially butterflies, bees, and beetles, is plentiful. Adapted for life among trees, jaguars and leopards are excellent climbers.

Forest floor

Very little light hits this level. Plant growth is minimal. Leaf litter covers the floor. Although decay is rapid in humid conditions, a low level of topsoil means it is low in nutrients.

Larger creatures live here. Giant anteaters, pumas, and gorillas inhabit this level. People also inhabit this level. When they clear land for farming, people quickly deplete the soil. As forest floor, there were few nutrients to begin with.

Compare and contrast forests

Below is a Venn diagram showing the similarities and differences between deciduous forests and tropical rain forests.

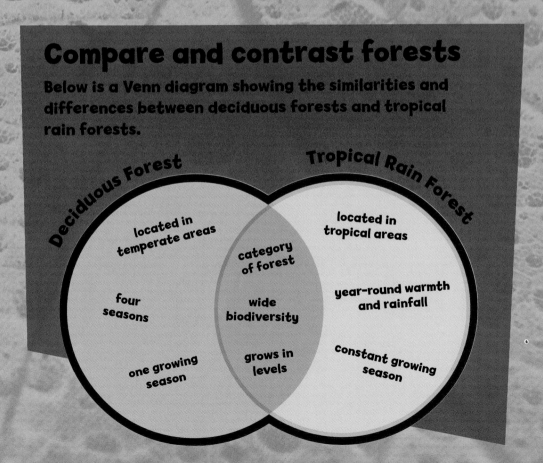

Deciduous Forest

Tropical Rain Forest

located in temperate areas

four seasons

one growing season

category of forest

wide biodiversity

grows in levels

located in tropical areas

year-round warmth and rainfall

constant growing season

TEMPERATE GRASSLANDS AND TROPICAL SAVANNAS

Depending on geography and climate, one biome may be much like another. Temperate grasslands and tropical savannas are very similar biomes. Look at the map on pages 6 and 7. How close are they to the equator?

Grasslands cover one-fifth of Earth's land surfaces. As with forests, grasslands are both temperate and tropical. Temperate grasslands and tropical savannas are the grassland biomes. Let's explore temperate grasslands first.

The grassy plains of South America are home to many animals, such as this Pampas cat.

Temperate grasslands

Locations:	Check the map on pages 6-7 to locate Australia, Canada, Eurasia, New Zealand, South America, and the United States.
Characteristics:	Hot summers and cold, dry winters; rich soil
Rainfall:	508 mm to 889 mm (20 to 35 inches)
Average Temperature:	10 °C (50 °F)
Threats:	Climate change, which leads to less rainfall, which leads to overgrazing (when grasslands die because too many animals are eating them)

Hot summers, cold winters

Temperate grasslands sprawl through Canada's prairies and the United States' plains. They spread out in South America's **pampas** (grassy plains) and Eurasia's **steppes** (large, treeless areas). <u>In the temperate zone, seasonal changes occur.</u> Summers are hot, while winters are cold. Temperatures range from –40 °C to 30 °C (–40 °F to 86 °F). But they've tipped the thermometer at well above 38 °C (100 °F). In late spring and early summer, the rainy season comes.

Grass, grass, and more grass

As the name indicates, grasses are the main plants in the temperate grassland. Grasses such as barley, buffalo grass, pampas grass, and wheat grow. Trees and shrubs are rare. With narrow leaves, plants are adapted to prevent water loss during dry seasons.

Fertile soil is jam-packed with nutrients from rotting roots. Deep and dark, soil allows vertical roots to anchor in the ground. Grazing animals can't yank deep roots from the soil.

Depending on the region, sunflowers, asters, and blazing stars bloom among grasses. In the United States' plains, blazing stars are adapted with spiky leaves to repel hungry **herbivores** (plant-eaters).

Butterflies sip nectar in blazing stars, but the plant's prickly leaves keep grazing cattle away.

Wide open spaces

Large grazing plant-eaters populate grasslands. For instance, wild horses, pronghorn, bison, and elk tromp through the plains of North America. Life in wide, open spaces is dangerous. Smaller mammals are vulnerable to roaming meat-eaters. Foxes, wolves, snakes, and coyotes hide easily in 2.5-meter (8-foot) grasses. Eagles, hawks, and owls are overhead threats.

BURROWS

Unlike forests, this environment offers few trees to scurry up for a quick escape. How do small mammals flee from predators? Mice, prairie dogs, and gophers have adapted. These rodents dig burrows. Sharp, curved claws and prominent front teeth are perfectly suited for tunneling underground. Some predators, though, are adapted for digging, too. Long weasels and stout badgers take off after rodents. They chase them into burrows and paw through the ground to dig them out.

CAMOUFLAGE

Grasshoppers and caterpillars, insect herbivores, find plenty to eat in grasslands. Both depend on camouflage to keep birds such as prairie chickens and bobolinks from devouring them. When it's time to lay eggs, a prairie chicken depends on another use of camouflage. She hides her nest in tall grasses, where it blends in with vegetation.

Did you know?

Prairie dogs aren't actually dogs. They're members of the rodent family, close relatives of squirrels. When settlers first explored the western United States, they encountered the rodents. Hearing the little critters' barking call, settlers dubbed the animals "prairie dogs."

When chased by a hungry predator, a prairie dog will make a run for the nearest burrow!

Savannas

Unlike temperate grasslands, savannas enjoy tropical climates. Savannas experience two seasons, a dry season and a rainy one. Rains pelt the savanna, sometimes severely, during a 6-month period. With them comes an incredible surge of growth. Then, drought takes over. Howling winds bring raging wildfires to the dry savanna. These wildfires encourage new growth, and the savanna continues to thrive.

Locations:	Check the map on pages 6–7 to find Australia, Africa, India, and South America.
Characteristics:	Two seasons, dry and rainy; annual drought; high **biodiversity**; porous soil
Rainfall:	508 mm–1,270 mm (20 to 50 inches)
Average Temperature:	10 °C (50 °F)
Threats:	Agriculture, grazing animals (overgrazing)

Africa's savannas

Africa's savannas boast high **biodiversity**. They are home to fierce **carnivores** such as lions and cheetahs. These beasts prey on hoofed herbivores like gazelles, wildebeests, and zebras. Hawks hover overhead with a birds-eye view of prey such as reptiles, rodents, and small mammals. Some of these animals, such as some species of reptile, are **omnivores**. Vultures swoop down to stuff themselves on carrion (rotting dead animals). Vultures are sloppy eaters. Adapted with featherless heads, the birds dive into dinner.

African elephants spend most of the day grazing. They are herbivores, but they rarely have to worry about natural predators!

PLANT ADAPTATIONS

You've learned grasslands are nearly treeless. In contrast, scattered trees and shrubs dot tropical savannas. Trees grow thick trunks like armor to battle wildfires. Plants' taproots (long, vertical roots) grow deep to search out water sources during drought. Soil is porous, which means it has many holes or spaces. It drains rapidly during rains.

Compare and contrast

Use the Venn diagram to review what you've learned about temperate grasslands and tropical savannas.

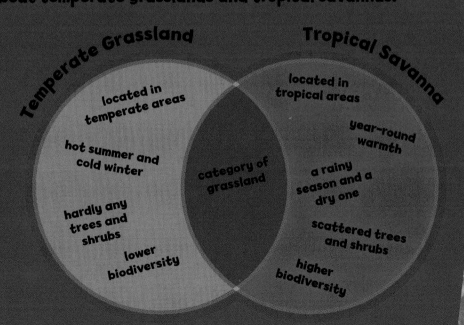

Temperate Grassland

Tropical Savanna

located in temperate areas

hot summer and cold winter

hardly any trees and shrubs

lower biodiversity

category of grassland

located in tropical areas

year-round warmth

a rainy season and a dry one

scattered trees and shrubs

higher biodiversity

The Desert

Earth's driest biome is the desert. Look at the map on pages 6 and 7. Which desert is closest to where you live? Very low rainfall characterizes Earth's driest biome. The desert receives less than 25 cm (10 inches) a year. Some rain evaporates before it sprinkles to the dry ground.

Deserts offer wild daily extremes in temperature. In the cloudless, **arid** environment, the Sun's heat escapes at night. Remember the forest biome's layers? With no canopy, as in the forest, sand is scorching hot in daytime. At night, its temperature plunges. There are few plants to trap heat and hold it at the ground.

Deserts cover around one-fifth of Earth's surface. In fact, deserts are Earth's fastest-growing biome. And that's not necessarily a good thing. Human activity, including overgrazing and land clearing, has caused damage.

Desertification

Desertification changes fertile land into dry land. Almost all plant life dies. How does it happen? An area's population booms. People's food needs explode. Farmers respond. They clear land for crops. Yet, when they do, farmers also remove vegetation that protects soil from **erosion**. Grazing animals are a problem, too. When animals graze repeatedly in one area, their sharp hooves batter and wear away soil.

Locations:	Look at the map on pages 6–7 to find Australia, Africa, India, Israel, Iraq, Mexico, and the southwest United States.
Characteristics:	Extreme changes in temperatures; very dry, rocky soil
Rainfall:	Less than 254 mm (10 inches)
Average Temperature:	38 °C (100 °F) during the day -4 °C (25 °F) at night
Threats:	Grazing animals, increased temperatures and wildfires due to climate change

You know biomes are related. Changes in one biome can create changes in others. Overgrazing animals, for example, can actually turn savannas into deserts.

Roasting hot temperatures in the day and freezing temperatures at night make deserts impossible for most plants and animals to survive in.

Adapted to drought and sandstorms

Desert soil is rocky, salty, and coarse. Plants endure extreme drought. How do they survive? With taproots and **pleated stems**. The crimson Sturt's Desert Pea is a protected plant that grows in South Australia. It relies on a taproot to seek groundwater and suck it up like a monster straw.

How are prickly cacti adapted? With stems pleated like accordions. When precious rain falls, pleats swell. They drink in water, stash it, and ration it during droughts. Waxy coverings on leaves and stems seal in moisture. That reduces **transpiration**, or water loss.

This purple prickly pear cactus is well equipped to survive the harsh conditions of the desert biome.

SHIPS OF THE DESERT

To survive in scorching heat, many desert animals are nocturnal. They're active in the cooler nights. Not camels. Called "ships of the desert," these pack animals are built for travel through sand. One adaptation is a triple set of eyelids. The top set is thin. It's see-through. A camel snaps it shut to battle sandstorms. Long, curly lashes fringe the other sets. They bat away gusting grains.

Camel humps weigh 36 kg (80 pounds). They're storage tanks for fat. Sometimes, when food is scarce, camels need to wait two weeks between meals.

Try this!

Compare transpiration

Water evaporates through transpiration. Follow these steps to compare . . .

⮕ You'll need gardening gloves, a cactus, plastic wrap or plastic bags, string, and a houseplant.

⮕ Put on the gloves. Then cover the cactus with plastic wrap or a bag. Tie the bottom with string. Repeat for the houseplant.

⮕ Place both plants in a sunny place. Wait 24 hours. Then remove the plastic wraps. Note how much moisture is on them. Which plant has lost less water?

Locations:	Check the map on pages 6-7 to find Alaska in the United States, northern Canada, northern Eurasia
Characteristics:	Harsh winters; permafrost; very short growing season; vegetation such as **lichens**, grasses, and shrubs; lower **biodiversity**
Rainfall:	150 to 250 mm (6 to 10 inches)
Average Temperature:	−40 °C to 18 °C (−40 °F to 65 °F)
Threats:	Air pollution, melting ice and permafrost from climate change, oil spills

<u>**What's Earth's coldest biome? The tundra. This biome experiences long, dark, frigid winters.**</u> **It's located in the Arctic and Antarctic, and also in some mountain regions, where the Sun's light and heat are limited. Temperatures are typically −4 °C to −14 °C (25 ° to 7 °F), but they can plummet to −55 °C (−67 °F).**

Permafrost

<u>**Permafrost characterizes the tundra.**</u> What is it? Exactly what it sounds like! Permafrost is a layer of permanently frozen soil and rock. It rests beneath the ground surface. The top layer of permafrost thaws in summer months. Yet, most of it stays frozen. The ground beneath never thaws.

EXTREME SURVIVORS

Even in one of Earth's coldest environments, species adapt and survive. In and around the Arctic tundra there are about 1,700 plant species! They are all able to resist violent winds and the cold, and can use short periods of sunlight to produce food.

Active layer

The top layer of permafrost is the active layer. When it melts, it provides an ecosystem for animals, plants, and insects. However, with Earth's warmer temperatures, the thaw depth has increased too much.

You've learned **desertification** changes biomes. The tundra is radically changing, too. Many scientists believe **global warming** is responsible. With a rising climate, permafrost breaks down. The dead plants and animals inside it **decompose**, releasing carbon dioxide gas (CO_2) into the atmosphere. That increases the **greenhouse effect**. The greenhouse effect is warmth from the Sun being trapped inside Earth's atmosphere.

The tundra transforms in summer. The active layer of permafrost melts. *See page 4 to see what winter tundra looks like!*

Adapted for brief growing seasons...

You know plants are the foundation of the food chain. The tundra's plants face Earth's shortest growing season. It's just 70 days. There's little time to make food. How do plants do it in such an inhospitable environment? They use **energy** effectively. Few trees grow. Instead, shrubs, lichens, grasses, and mosses stay small. They grow close to the ground.

Plants can't establish a deep, vertical root system in rigid permafrost. Instead, they thrive with a shallow, horizontal system. Consider the cheery Arctic poppy. This survivor is a **heliotrope**. It aims its petals toward the Sun. When the Sun moves, the poppy's face and leaves move with it. The better to catch rays. The poppy sets roots between rocks. Why? Rocks absorb solar energy. In the poppy's cup, insects such as gnats and midges bask in warmth.

The Sun won't be out for long, so the Arctic poppy takes full advantage of the light and warmth it provides.

...And bitter temperatures

Blubber, a thick layer of fat, is an **adaptation** for warm-blooded animals such as polar bears and seals. Their body temperatures remain almost constant. Blubber is essential for survival in bitter temperatures. Have you bundled up in a bulky parka in cold weather? Blubber insulates in the same way.

Woolly coats protect animals, too. Thick fur or hair provides warmth for polar bears, musk ox, caribou, Arctic foxes, and Arctic wolves. Did you know polar bears have two coats of transparent (see-through) fur? The undercoat is thick. Over it, the guard coat contains clear, hollow hairs. When the Sun's light reflects on the coat, our eyes view it as white.

Compare and contrast

Use the Venn diagram to review what you've learned about the desert and the tundra.

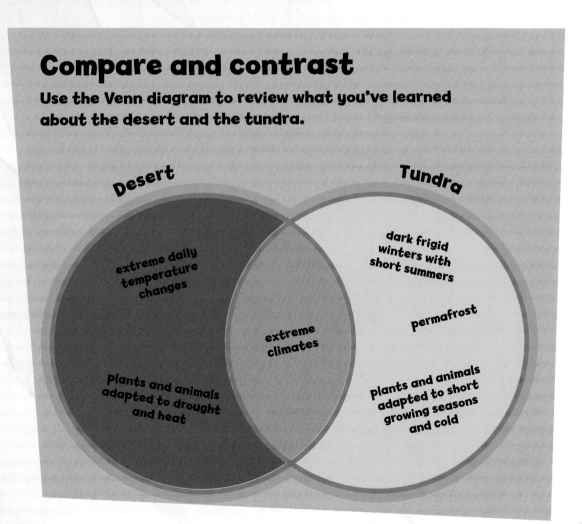

Desert

Tundra

extreme daily temperature changes

dark frigid winters with short summers

extreme climates

permafrost

plants and animals adapted to drought and heat

plants and animals adapted to short growing seasons and cold

Marine Regions

You've learned about Earth's **terrestrial biomes**. Now, discover the aquatic biome, which reaches from the North Pole to the South. <u>**The aquatic biome includes two categories, marine and freshwater.**</u> What makes them different? The amount of salt they contain. Oceans are approximately 3 percent to 3.4 percent salt.

Saltwater marine biomes

Earth is a watery planet. Oceans and seas cover nearly 75 percent of its surface. Saltwater marine biomes encircle every continent. They include the Arctic, Atlantic, Indian, Pacific, and Southern Oceans. Marine biomes contain a whopping 97 percent of Earth's water.

Depending on location, oceans experience different climates. Temperatures vary greatly. For instance, polar waters plunge to an icy −2 °C (28 °F). Tropical waters can be as warm as 36 °C (97 °F).

Light penetration

You know sunlight penetrates different levels of land biomes. Sunlight breaks through water, too. As waters get deeper, levels of light penetration become lower. In deeper waters, temperatures decrease, too. Scientists divide the ocean into zones, or levels. Take a look at the panel on the next page to find out more.

Did you know?

The Southern Ocean is Earth's "newest" ocean. In 2000 scientists renamed the southern parts of the Atlantic, Indian, and Pacific oceans as the Southern Ocean. Full of gigantic icebergs, the ocean surrounds Antarctica. It's double the size of the United States.

Deeper and darker

Plants depend on sunlight to perform **photosynthesis**. Algae and seagrass live in the sunlight zone's warm waters. In this bright zone, the ocean's **biodiversity** is highest. That's why coral reefs are sometimes called "rain forests of the sea." Animal life is plentiful and active. Large fish, such as shark and tuna, inhabit this zone. So do smaller fish, including blowfish and clownfish, sea turtles, lobsters, crabs, and seals.

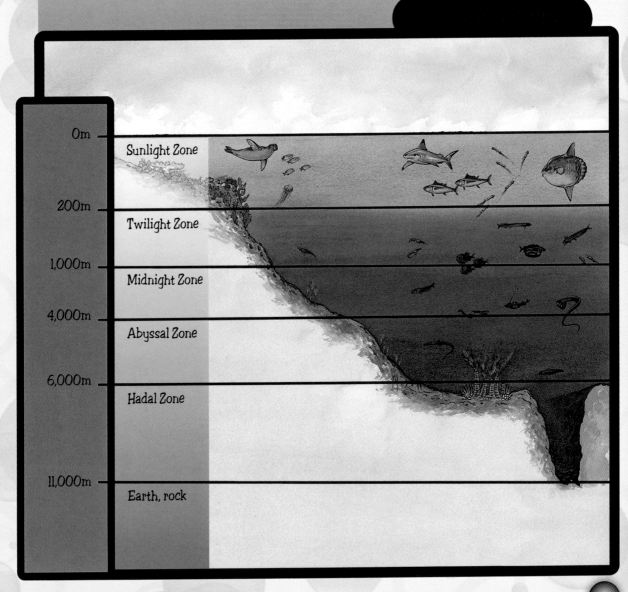

0m	Sunlight Zone
200m	Twilight Zone
1,000m	Midnight Zone
4,000m	Abyssal Zone
6,000m	Hadal Zone
11,000m	Earth, rock

Adapted to life underwater

Ocean waters move constantly. Tides ebb and flow. Waves crash against shores. As fish swim, they adapt to water temperatures. How do they do it? Fish are cold-blooded. Their body temperatures change depending on their surroundings.

Antifreeze proteins

You know blubber insulates warm-blooded animals from cold. Without protective fat, how do fish keep from freezing to death in icy seas? They use what scientists call "antifreeze proteins." These proteins found in blood clamp onto ice crystals in fish blood. Proteins keep the ice crystals from getting larger and hurting the fish.

Shaped for survival

Meet the Tiger of the Sea, the brutal barracuda. This cold-blooded predator is built for survival in coral reefs. How? The fish is missile-shaped. It zips through coral easily. Protruding, razor-sharp teeth allow it to snatch and kill its prey.

The barracuda's teeth are built for snatching prey.

Bioluminescence

How do some deep-sea creatures find their ways in dark waters? With **bioluminescence** (light made by a creature's body). Through this **adaptation**, animals use chemicals or bacteria inside their bodies to glow. Sea creatures light paths to see. They keep predators away and help to attract mates. Check out the bizarre-looking female deep-sea angler fish. She totes a built-in fishing pole. A luminescent spine dangles from her snout. Unsuspecting prey head for the light—and then into a huge mouth.

The female angler fish carries a luminescent fishing pole.

Shaded for survival

The shark, another toothy predator, has special coloring. It's darker on the top than on the bottom. What happens when prey peeks down at the shark? The shark blends with dark waters. Yet, when prey is below it, the shark's lighter bottom camouflages it against brighter waters.

FRESHWATER REGIONS

Lakes and ponds, rivers and streams, and wetlands comprise Earth's freshwater regions. Unlike oceans, they contain very little salt. Levels are typically less than 1 percent salt.

In freshwaters the current, or steady movement of water, varies. In lakes and ponds, waters have little or slow movement. Sometimes, the surface water doesn't move at all. Yet, weather conditions, like winds and storms, can turn lake waters choppy. In some rivers and streams, water rushes.

Estuaries

Estuaries are the lower areas of rivers, where tides roll in. They're located near the coast, close to oceans and seas.

Sheltered waters

Estuaries are found around the globe. In these sheltered waters, animals and plants thrive. Young animals grow up far from ocean predators. Waters are packed with decaying materials. Soil is full of nutrients. It allows plants to grow in abundance. The plants provide plenty of food for animal **consumers**, including worms, sea birds, raccoons, and reptiles. All animals are consumers because they eat plants or they eat other animals that ate plants. Because of this, plants are called **producers**.

Destination spots

Have you ever visited an estuary? Residents sail, swim, and fish, while drinking in local wildlife. Visitors enjoy estuaries, too. Tampa Bay, Florida, is a popular destination for visitors from around the world. People enjoy photographing protected manatees, ghost crabs, and burrowing owls.

Did you know?

Estuaries battle water pollution. They filter sediments, dirt, and junk before they pour into larger bodies of water.

In estuaries, crashes with people's boats and fishing nets endanger manatees.

In estuaries, freshwater and saltwater mingle in increasingly higher amounts. They are divided into three zones.

ZONE ONE
In the first zone, a river first touches saltwater. Most water is freshwater.

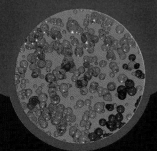

ZONE TWO
In the second zone, freshwater and saltwater are equal.

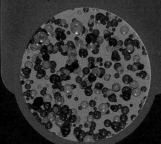

ZONE THREE
In the third zone, the river pours into the ocean. Saltwater is present.

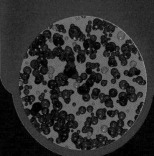

Adapted for mingled waters

Water plants such as algae and seaweed aren't true plants. They don't have roots, stems, or leaves. Yet, they still perform **photosynthesis**. How? Seaweed and algae take in nutrients directly from water. They obtain carbon dioxide from water, rather than air.

Pretty flowering water lilies float on the surface of the water. They look like they're not attached to anything. Yet, long stems are adapted to a watery home. They stretch all the way down to the bottom. Roots anchor the lily.

Great blue herons and great egrets wander estuaries. The heron's spindly legs are an **adaptation** for moving through shoreline waters. The egret's pointy bill is perfect for catching fish.

Bogs

Bogs and swamps are other wetlands. Like estuaries, they are found all over the world. They contain only freshwater.

Bogs grow over sphagnum moss, which holds water. **Peat** is a major feature of these waterlogged areas. Peat consists of tightly packed decayed matter. It's usually soaked with water.

Bogs depend on **precipitation** for water. Bog waters are **acidic** (have the properties of acid), and soil is low in nutrients. Some plants grow, including cranberries, mosses, and shrubs. Others perform an extreme adaptation to survive. Carnivorous plants such as pitcher plants capture insects and digest them. for nutrients.

Did you know?

The pitcher plant lures insects with nectar. An insect looking for a taste of the nectar finds a slippery surface on the edge of the plant's jug-shaped leaves. It falls into the plant's "pitcher," where rainwater has collected. Here the insect drowns and the plant goes to work slowly digesting the body!

Swamps

Swamps are different than other wetland regions and support greater **biodiversity**. Their soil is rich with nutrients. Trees, shrubs, and woody plants grow. Food is everywhere. Birds, fish, crayfish, and clams find plenty to eat.

Alligators, which can weigh a ton, top the swamp food chain. In muddy swamps, alligators blend right in. They are adapted for hunting in water. Alligators snatch prey and hold it underwater until the prey dies. How do alligators do it without drowning? They tightly close their throats.

Alligators capture and drown prey—without drowning themselves.

Drained and cleared

Bogs provide peat for fuel, while swamps supply building materials. Unfortunately, many wetlands have been drained and cleared over the years. People have used the land for mining and agriculture.

Logging: A Threat to Sea Creatures?

Can logging rainforests on land cause trouble for sea creatures? Definitely, say researchers.

A wilderness wonderland

Pongara Beach National Park in Gabon is a wilderness wonderland. The park is comprised of different habitats. With rainforests, **savannas**, swamps, and lakes, it stretches across the Atlantic coast. Visitors gawk at amazing scenery. They observe chimpanzees, hippos, elephants, and bush pigs in their natural habitats. Within the park is Pongara Beach, a protected nesting area for critically endangered leatherback turtles.

Lost logs

During breeding seasons, leatherback turtles leave the sea to lay eggs on land. How does logging hurt their progress? When people clear rainforests, they transport logs by floating them through water. In the process, some logs get lost or ditched. The stragglers wander out to sea. Eventually, hundreds of logs wash up on shore and clutter beaches.

Blocked paths

Researchers believe about 14 percent of nesting attempts fail because of logs. Slow movers on land, turtles lumber over sands. With logs blocking their paths, turtles can't reach nesting areas. Confused, some turtles give up the long trek and head back to sea. Others lay eggs close to the shoreline—but seawater kills eggs. Sadly, some turtles get trapped inside piles of logs and die.

Helping an endangered species

This critically endangered species faces threats from fishing practices and habitat destruction. Now, it also encounters new threats from logging. Researchers hope environmental groups will band together to tackle the problem. Clearing logs from shorelines will help, they believe. Researchers also point out the bigger picture. They say it's critical to change logging practices and address the waste of our precious natural resources, on land and at sea.

A critically endangered leatherback turtle travels to a protected nesting area.

MEET THE TOLLUND MAN!
THE WORLD'S MOST FAMOUS BOG MUMMY

Bog mummies of men, women, and children have been discovered throughout Europe. Long ago, when ancient people buried bodies in bogs, they dug shallow graves in **peat**. They drained water and placed bodies inside. Water filled the graves. It completely covered bodies.

Acidic bog waters kill bacteria. So buried bodies become amazingly well preserved. Tanned and leathery, these extraordinary bodies provide valuable clues to the past.

The Tollund Man

In 1950, two brothers from Tollund, Denmark, worked in a peat bog. As they dug for fuel, they happened upon a shocking sight—a dead body! They called the authorities, who called archaeologists. Archaeologists are scientists who study artifacts (objects) from the past. They learn about ancient cultures and their ways of life. And death!

What did scientists learn?

Archaeologists named the bog mummy the Tollund Man. His face was so well preserved, they could see reddish whiskers and frown lines. They spotted eyebrows and eyelashes, too. Archaeologists believe the Tollund Man's body is 2,400 years old. At the time of death he was around 40. By examining the contents of his stomach, scientists learned his last meal had been vegetarian soup!

The Tollund Man lived during the Iron Age, when most people were farmers. With a noose still around his neck, the Tollund Man was probably hanged from a tree. After his death, someone cut down his body and respectfully closed his eyes and mouth. This indicates the Tollund Man may have been sacrificed to the gods.

Where is he now?

The Tollund Man is on display at Denmark's Silkeborg Museum. People from all over can visit and marvel at this well preserved human who died 2,400 years ago.

WHAT DO YOU KNOW ABOUT BIOMES?

1 What is the range of living things in a community called?
a neighborhood
b bioluminescence
c adaptation
d biodiversity

2 The top level of the deciduous forest is called what?
a understory
b canopy
c ceiling
d forest top

3 A temperate climate experiences what?
a four clear seasons
b a rainy season and a dry season
c cold temperatures all year
d hot temperatures all year

4 When an animal goes dormant for the winter, it?
a dies
b camouflages
c migrates
d hibernates

5 Which of the following is a measure of typical weather patterns in an area over a certain period?
a temperature
b climate
c season
d biome

6 Deep-water fish are adapted for life in darkness through what?
a blubber
b saltwater
c bioluminescence
d hibernation

7 Freshwater and saltwater meet where?
a in coral reefs
b in rivers
c in lakes
d in estuaries

Check your answers on page 47!

Glossary

acid rain rain containing harmful chemicals. Air pollution from cars, factories, and other polluters mixes with the water vapor in rain clouds. The rain is damaging to the environment.

acidic forming acid

adaptation special characteristics that make a plant or animal suited for survival in its environment

arid extremely dry

biodiversity range of living things in a community, ecosystem, biome, or even the entire world

bioluminescence creation of light in the bodies of living creatures

biome one of Earth's large physical areas with a particular geography and climate

carnivore a meat-eating animal

cell basic unit of life

chlorophyll a green chemical in plants

coniferous characterized by cone-bearing trees

consumer creature that feeds on producers (all animals are consumers)

deciduous having leaves that fall off seasonally

decompose when fungi, bacteria, and insects eat wastes and break down nutrients from the dead

desertification the process, often through human activity, of turning fertile land into desert

dormant an inactive, sleep-like state

ecosystem a group of living and nonliving things that exist in the same environment and rely on one another for survival

energy what is produced when cells break down and change food molecules through chemical reactions

erosion a wearing away of soil and rocks

extinct when a plant or animal species is completely wiped out. It will never be back again.

global warming gradual rise of average temperatures across Earth

greenhouse effect trapping of heat in Earth's atmosphere, as caused by carbon dioxide and other gases

heliotrope a plant that turns toward the Sun

herbivore a plant-eating animal

hibernate to become dormant in the winter and live off stored fat

lichen fungi and algae combined to make a plant. Lichens typically grow on rocks and trees.

migrate to move from one area to another, especially during winter

mining when people dig underground to find resources such as coal or valuable minerals

omnivore an animal that eats both plants and animals

pampas treeless, grassy plains in South America

pasture grassy land for grazing animals to feed

peat tightly packed decayed plant material found in bogs

permafrost layer of frozen soil and rock just beneath the ground's surface

photosynthesis process by which plants use energy from the Sun to make food from raw materials

pleated stems an adaptation featuring folds that hold water

precipitation water that falls to Earth. It can be in any form, such as rain or snow.

producer organism that makes its own food. Almost all plants are producers.

savanna grassland in a tropical climate

steppes large treeless areas in Eurasia

symbiotic relationship when two plants or animals live together in a relationship that is a benefit to at least one of them

temperate areas with a temperate climate have four seasons and a range of weather conditions throughout the year

terrestrial on land. For example, tundra is a terrestrial biome.

transpiration loss of water vapor from plants' leaves

Find Out More

Books

Allaby, Michael. **Deserts**. New York: Chelsea House, 2006.

Bright, Michael. **Changing Ecosystems**. Chicago: Heinemann Library, 2009.

Freedman, Jeri. **Grasslands**. New York: Rosen 2009.

Townsend, John. **Predicting the Effects of Climate Change**. Chicago: Heinemann Library, 2009.

Websites

http://pbskids.org/zoom/activities/sci//biomeinabaggie.html
Learn how to grow your own biomes in plastic bags!

http://www.woodland-trust.org.uk/garden/
Explore a virtual garden to find out how climate change can affect everything living there.

http://earthobservatory.nasa.gov/Laboratory/Biome/
Investigate Earth's terrestrial biomes.

Places to visit

The Field Museum
1400 S. Lake Shore Drive
Chicago, IL 60605

Phone: (312) 922-9410
http://www.fieldmuseum.org

Smithsonian National Museum of Natural History
10th Street and constitution Ave., NW
Washington, D.C. 20560

Phone: (202) 633-1000
http://mnh.si.edu

Quiz answers

1. d, **2.** b, **3.** a, **4.** d, **5.** b, **6.** c, **7.** d.

Index